THE STEVINGTON HISTORICAL

IN ASSOCIATION WITH

ROGER DAY

STEVINGTON IN PICTURES

MMIV

ISBN: 0-9540703-2-1

Published by the Stevington Historical Trust, designed and set in Palatino Linotype by Roger Day and printed in Great Britain by Ian Allan Printing Ltd, Hersham, Surrey KT12 4RG

The Team

Acknowledgements

We should like to thank the following who supplied photographs and assisted with the production of the text: Simon and Kathy Brown, Joyce and Jim Cooke, Alan Cox, Ray Cox, Barbara and Ken Davies, James Day, Rev Dennis Dessert, Marion Field, Rhiannon Fraser, Gary Harber, Bill Harris, Isobel Hart, Marion Hext, Dita Hollins, Ralph Jeffries, Jim Keech, Dennis King, David Litchfield, Sally MacDonald, Mary Mackness, Marina Markham, John Moore, Angela Parker, Ken Prentice, Michael Read, Michael Robinson, Robert Shaftoe, George Strong, Stan Walker, Bernard West, Bill Wills-Moren, Frank Wooding.

Verses by Peter (Rhymin') Stileman

Abbreviations

Village History: *Stevington: The Village History (2001)*
RDC   Bedford Rural District Council
PCC   Parochial Church Council

Index

Subscription List

Vivien and Colin Aspley
Mr and Mrs Baillie
Di and Laurie Bailey
Helen Barrett (2)
Dinah and David Bate (2)
Bedfordshire County Council (2)
Jean and Richard Blayney
Sharon and Seb Blore-Rimmer
Marion and Tom Batty
Betty and Reg Bishop
Philip Bond
Chris Boniface
Beth Breen
Sarah and Mike Bush (2)
Barabara and Brian Cattermole
Nigel Chadburn
Daphne Chivers
Lief and Lynn Christison, Bedford
Avis Clayton
Don Cleal
Barbara Collins
Debbie and Robert Collins (3)
Jeff Comb
Margaret and Terry Compton
Caroline and Peter Conquest
Sheila and Steve Cowley
Liz and Tim Cox
Ray Cox (2)
John Crookall, Harrold
Judith Cummings
Barbara and Ken Davies
Rebecca Dean
Diane Disson
anne Dodd
Heather and Bob Eadie
Chris Easton
Alan Edwards, Bedford (5)
Joan Edmunds, Eastbourne (2)
Sandra Fellows
Marion Field
Jen and Charles Finch
Chris and Richard Galley
Karen and Geoff Gallimore, Ipswich
Sylvia Goddard
Angie and Mike Grafton (3)
Anna and Bob Hart
Joan and Peter Hart (5)
Marion and Terry Hext
Frances and John Hirst
Franie Hodgkinson
Dita and Tony Hollins (3)
M I Hoxey, Kempston
Pauline Indge

Margaret and Peter Jackson
Anne and Lawrence Kay
Annette and Richard Keech, Brogborough
Cynthia and Roy Keech
Peter Knight
Magnus and Tricia Lennie
David Litchfield
Sally and Malcolm Macdonald (2)
Mary Mackness (5)
Marina and Albert Markham
Alma Mayes (3)
Pippa and Paul Middleton (3)
John Moore
Iain Morrison
Sue and Jim Novis
Anna and Simon O'Connor
Heather and Keith Parkinson
Joan Pearson (3)
Jacqui and Bryan Pell (3)
Doreen and Sid Pendlington
Roger and Linda Penney
Sally and James Petre (2)
Ian and Pat Pickup
Madge and Ken Prentice
Sandra and Alan Proud
Margaret and Roy Pryn
Linda and Michael Purser, Bedford
Denise and Ron Randall, Bedford
Judith and Michael Robinson
Ilse and John Rogers
Bill Seamarks
David Seamarks, Oakley (2)
Ann and Roger Seaton (3)
Robert Shaftoe (2)
Stewart and Sarah Short
Mick Stalley
Liz and Brian Stammers (3)
Rosemary and David Stanbridge
Ann and Peter Stileman (6)
Terry Studley
Sue and Chris Thornton
Connie and Stan Walker (2)
E I Walker, Kempston
E R Walker, Kempston (2)
Jeanette and James Wannerton
Anne and David Warburton (3)
Jacqui and John Ward
Mary and Brian Webb
R M Webb, Isle of Man
Ralph Weedon, Glasgow (2)
Joan and Bill Wills-Moren (3)
Daphne and Tom Wooding
Sue and Andrew Young

List of Photographs

Good Morning Stevington

Stevington, Goodnight!

Foreword

Since Henry Fox-Talbot pioneered photography in 1839 Stevington has changed a little, to say the least. Up to the First World War and beyond a camera was an expensive luxury and Stevington was not a well-off community. When we of the Historical Trust decided that we would collect and publish as many photographs as we could to illustrate how the Village has changed, we found old pictures hard to come by.

However, in regard to the contemporary scene we were more fortunate in that three years ago Roger Day started to compile a photographic record of the Village and, having seen some examples of his work, we had no hesitation in asking him to help us. The result has been a brilliant series of images of contemporary Stevington.

For the old photographs which appear here I have to thank all those Villagers who have lent us pictures. For the new images we have to thank Roger Day who has dedicated his contribution to the memory of his daughter, Lizzy. We hope you will be fascinated by the old ones and enchanted by the new.

I should confess to one liberty we have taken. The observant reader will find many references to Picts Hill. A boundary change in 1946 moved that area from Stevington to Turvey. Why, no-one can remember. The lost land includes Moat Farm and Picts Hill House. For historical completeness we have included pictures of Picts Hill here.

I must also record the generosity of Stevington Parish Council which made us a handsome grant and loan which made this publication possible. The Council's support has been a great spur to us as has been the willingness of all the subscribers to take us on trust.

We are grateful to Peter Conquest and Terry Studley who read the proofs, though of course any errors are the responsibility of the Trust.

David Stanbridge

Duck End Farm

October 2004

Good Morning, Stevington!

Introduction

Stevington lies five miles west of Bedford in the valley of the Great Ouse River. It looks across to Pavenham and Oakley on the other side. It is in the northern lee of the escarpment which carries the A428 Bedford to Northampton trunk road.

Historically, Stevington is an archetypal Anglo-Saxon Village. However, apart from St Mary's Church, the tower of which is Saxon, there is little building in the Village that predates the early 17th Century. The Vicarage is an exception, and possibly parts of Duck End Farm and Meeting Farm. The stone buildings of the 17th and 18th Centuries which give the Village its character were built of the local oolitic limestone. Brick was not used until the 19th Century, when slate also became available through the canal system.

The Village's rural scene dates from the Enclosure Award of 1806. The modern development took place first of all between the two World Wars, mostly in Court Lane; then in the late 1960s and early 1970s with Burridge's Close and Farley Way, and latterly in 1999 with Foxbrook.

In *Stevington: The Village History* we remarked how the Village has constantly adapted to change over the centuries. Amazingly, it has continued to do so. Even in the face of the rural deprivation of the last 30 years, which has hit Stevington as hard as any other Village, it has maintained its sense of community; and that vibrancy is something which strikes many visitors to the Village.

You cannot escape it if you live here. Why this should be so is difficult to pinpoint, and it would take a complex sociological study to understand it. We can only count ourselves lucky and hope that it continues.

Chapter 1   Landscape and Seasons

'Tis common knowledge that a witness is more stirred
By brilliant image than by any word;
So scan these views of nature flourishing:
The river flowing and the Bluebell Wood in spring.

The River Great Ouse marking the boundary where once the Danelaw terminated and Anglo-Saxon England began, is probably the feature of the landscape which has changed least over the years. However, the fields and woodland we see now are very different from those which the Domesday Book commissioners encountered in 1086. The Enclosure Award of 1806 laid the foundation for today's field and road scene and swept away the open fields of mediaeval times. **Plate 3** is a plan drawn by Bernard West in 1943 showing the layout of the Village. **Plate 4**, an aerial photograph of 1935, illustrates the plan. **Plate 5** is the same view today and **Plate 6** shows the whole Village in its rural setting. This provides a rich backcloth to the four seasons.

Spring, the season of renewal, is featured most memorably in the romantic sight of the bluebell wood at Woodcraft **[7]**. At this time the Village decks itself in colour, as this picture of Park Road demonstrates **[9]**, or shrouds the early walker in morning mist **[1]**. The new growth soon gathers pace and in **Plate 2** the trees on either side of Park Road form a leafy entrance arch at the eastern end of the Village.

Later, in summer, the butterbur and roses flourish below St Mary's **[11]** while dots of poppies sprinkle their scarlet among the farmers' crops **[12]**. The odiferous rape encircles the Village in a halo of yellow **[8]**. Meanwhile, the Great Ouse mirrors a riot of skies, green banks and trees as it glides and meanders slowly towards Bedford **[13 and 14]**. The hatch of mayflies in glorious sunlight **[10]** delights the fisherman's eye and turns his thoughts to salmon and trout in vain, as there are none in our river. However, not all is calm at this time of year; the summer storm provides a tumultuous contrast **[20 and 21]**.

Autumn, with its amazing and indescribable colours **[24-6]** and extraordinary skies **[22]** competes in beauty with all that has gone before **[15]**. Even stubble from the harvest presents an artistic prospect for the camera **[16]**; then the ploughshare churns up the earth to substitute a rival scene **[17]**. The countryside, usually dry at this time of year, provides ideal conditions for the walker **[18 and 19]**, while the Ouse reflects the autumn tints of its bankside trees **[27]**. A leaf-strewn Park Road, appeals to the photographer's eye as it curves by Farley Way, **[23]**, while the moon holds its pose for him **[32]**. Autumn is also the season of marvellous sunsets **[28-31]**.

Winter, inevitably, gives the Village a sad look but with the trees shorn of their leaves **[34]** the Ouse maintains its varied appeal even in flood **[33 and 35]**. When it snows the prospect of the *Red Lion* is transformed **[36]**, as is the view of the Cross with Silver Street behind **[37]**. When finally it stops snowing the whole Silver Street and Park Road vista appears **[38-40]**.

1   Misty Morning

2   The Eastern Approaches

4 Aerial View of the Village in 1935, Looking North-East

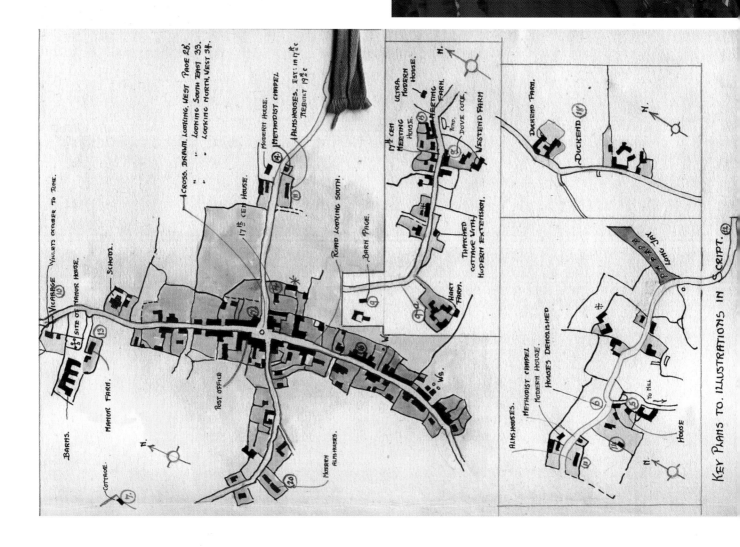

6   The Curvature of the Earth: The Village in its Hinterland

7   Bluebell Wood in Full Bloom

8   Yellow Peril

9   Park Road in Spring

10   The Mayfly Hatch

11   Butterbur and Roses

12   Poppies for Remembrance

13   Levels of the Great Ouse Looking Downstream to Oakley

14   Great Ouse: Trees and Reflections

15   Ripe for Harvest

16   The Shaven Stubble

17   Plough Lines Weaving

18   Country Walk

19   The Way to Walk or Ride

22   The Early Autumn Skyline

23 Shuffle Through the Leaves

24 Berry Ripe

27   Autumn View of the River

28   Sunset Boulevard

29   Red Sky at Night, Photographer's Delight

30   What Does This Portend? The End of the World?

31   The Windmill at Sunset

34 Sunlight and Shadow

32 Autumn Moon

33 The Ouse Bursting Its Banks

35   Levels of the Swollen River

36   The *Lion* in Winter

38   Park Road Piste

37   The "Spike" in a Blizzard

40   Budd's
     Hill Run

39   Snowbound
     Silver Street

Chapter 2   Farming and Animals

The crowded farmyard featured once, and now,
The rampant bull midst massive tons of cow.
Alas, big business now is often that
Of the inseminator in a bowler hat.

Until the Second World War agriculture was the main occupation in the Village, though between the Wars the numbers working on the land in the Parish fell by 50%. The smallholdings have all but disappeared but there are still seven active farms in the Village. They are mostly worked by their owners. However, the only working farmers resident in the Parish are David Stanbridge (see Chapter 6 **361**) at Duck End Farm, Brian and Damian Pell **[53]**, who together work Mill Farm, and Peter Brown at Tythe Farm. Frank Wooding (see Chapter 7 **466**) was the last manager at Hart Farm. The Day family farms at Picts Hill.

Between the wars the whole family as well as the farm labourers would be involved in stacking wheat sheaves **[45]** and haymaking **[46]**. On the other hand there were times of the year when even for a farmer it was possible to relax and put your feet up **[41 and 42]**.

Two ploughs illustrate the transition from horse to mechanization. **Plate 43** is a horse drawn plough of about 1880. **Plate 44** is a tractor-drawn plough of the 1920s. **Plate 47** is an early photograph showing the power of steam thrashing. **Plate 48** shows Ken Prentice with his combine, a Minneapolis Moline, reputed to be the first in the Village, just after the Second World War. Finally, a spectacle to wonder at: mechanisation in action and the camera's brilliance in capturing what a tractor driver has to endure when drilling dry earth **[49 and 50]**. And nowadays there is harvesting at night, something not possible before mechanisation **[51 and 52]**. On the other hand, an early picture of farm animals **[54]** presents much the same scene as today **[55]**.

However, fifty or sixty years ago it was the custom to take the odd cow or heifer to fulfil an appointment with the nearest bull **[57-60]**. This inevitably meant a journey through the Village. As the bewildered animal was not led by a halter (first catch your cow) fun was guaranteed. The smallest boy was sent ahead to close the garden gates, which were promptly opened again by the goodwife outraged by such a liberty. The cow would trot happily along, but unable to resist an open gate, would

investigate. This would result in the goodwife emerging from the back door brandishing a besom whereupon the startled cow would embark on a high speed tour of the garden collecting some washing on the way. The delighted drover's cup was overflowing when the cow emerged onto the road with a pair of voluminous unmentionables attached to its horn. In modern times we have the artificial inseminator, otherwise known as "the bull in the bowler hat", which is the most these cows can hope for **[56]**.

The days of farm horses are also over, as we are reminded by the pictures of a farm worker pausing to pay tribute on the day of King George V's funeral **[62]**. This fine shire dwarfs a young Stan Walker **[64]**. An earlier photograph depicts Horace Prentice of Meeting Farm showing off his fine horse which no doubt also pulled his trap **[63]**. An old picture taken outside the Almshouses **[61]** has George Seamarks on the left, identified by his "stiff" knee. He overcame his disability remarkably well and was able to do most jobs on the farm as well as the next man. His injury was caused by falling out of an upstairs window.

The days of the horse were not always as golden as we like to imagine and horses caused many injuries and deaths. Nowadays the horse is for recreation **[65 and 66]**. Nor must we forget the donkey, Melissa, so popular with generations of schoolchildren who fed her as they passed the field adjacent to the Church Rooms on their way to and from school **[83]**. He is ridden here by Matthew Seager.

It is said that "cats look down on us; dogs look up to us; but pigs is equal". The huge boar, Halesfarm Field Marshall 110, captured in **Plate 67** surely looks down on us. After all, he travelled by rail all the way from Bedford to Oakley in 1957 as the sole passenger en route to Duck End Farm. The photograph of Brian Pell's breeding stock **[68]** reminds us that there are pigs in Stevington no more.

An early picture **[69]** shows one of the Turney brothers feeding his sheep, probably at Moat Farm which they owned with Duck End Farm. You can just make out the ridge and furrow and the horse and cart on the right. Nowadays the only sheep in Stevington are owned outside the Village and graze on leased pasture [70-74].

There may still be some turkeys in the Village but not kept on the free-range scale of Dorothy Robinson of Hart Farm in the 1930s, shown in **Plate 76** with old Shipley. The goose-stepping geese in **Plate 77** are definitely free-range though the Canada geese look more sedate [91]. In contrast, the hen in the armchair in **Plate 75** has a more liberal idea of the concept of free range. The friendship of a cat and dog in **Plate 84** one hundred years ago is little different from that of their successors today.

Then there are the wolves [85, 87 and 88]. They must have been absent from the Village for over a thousand years. In those days they were rather more menacing than their friendly and well-fed descendants kept in a secure compound at Moat Farm. Other wolves take liberties [100]. Incidentally, no-one asked the deer [81 and 82] what they thought about the introduction of the enemy. In **Plate 78** Barry Compton shows off another predator as does Ken Ward in **Plate 79**. In contrast the doves in **Plate 80** send a different message. Sadly, their owner has gone but the doves remain in mourning.

The non-domestic animals of the Parish lend their own touch of beauty. There have been swans on the Ouse here as long as anyone can remember [94] and the goldfinch [93] was undoubtedly here before us, but other animals are rather more recent additions to this locality [89 and 90]. Some birds make themselves at home in or on our homes [97 and 98], while others eat the newly sown seed. The scarecrow [99] cannot compete effectively with the gas gun and it's time to go when the food has run out and the nights get chilly [95 and 96]. Meanwhile, the ubiquitous rabbit does its best to reduce the farmers' profits [86] as does the hungry pheasant [92], while the butterbur finds a novel visitor [101].

41 Eddy and Amos
Turney Shifting th[e]
Deck with a Frien[d]
from Chicheley be[fore]
the First World W[ar]

42 The End of
the Day for
Amos Turney

43 Horse-Drawn Plough c. 1880

44 Tractor-Drawn Plough c. 1920

45   Stacking Wheat Sheaves in a Round Stack

46   The Hay Wain: Brenda Stanbridge and Alf Swain

47   Steam Threshing
     c. 1910

48   Ken Prentice with
     Combine c. 1948

49   Drilling with Dust

50   Seeding with More Dust

51   The Night Shift

52   More Night Work

53   Damian, Jacqui and Brian Pell

54 At Rest in Home Field, Duck End Farm. A Nondescript Herd of Short-Horns c. 1910

55 A Similar Scene Today at Hart Farm

56 Subjects for big Business?

57   Enter Big Business

Getting Amongst Them

59   Enter Bigger Business

60   Bigger Business Sizes Up a Mate

61   Horse and Foals outside
      the Almshouses: George
      Seamarks on the Left

62   Old Shipley
      Remembers:
      The Funeral of
      King George V

63   Horace Prentice with his Fine Horse

64   A Young Stan Walker Riding High

65   Not Quite Banbury

66   Horses under the Rainbow

67 Halesfarm Field
Marshall 110: Hero of
the Great Train Ride

68   Pigs at Mill Far

69   Eddy Turney Feeding Sheep at Moat Farm c. 1910.

70   There's Still a Future
for Mint Sauce

71   Horned Sheep
at Pond Farm

72   Come and
     Get It!

73   Now You've Got It!

74   We're Late;
     We're Late!

75 When Little Hen Oh When
When, When Will You Lay
Me an Egg for My Tea?
Duck End Farm c. 1910

76 Dorothy Robinson
and Old Shipley at the
Christmas Round-Up

77 Well They Saved Rom
Did They Not?

78   Barry Compton Shows off his Harris' Hawks

79   Ken Ward with His Hawk

80   Lovey Dovey

81   Deer at Picts Hill

82   Early Doors at the Pond

83 Melissa Ridden by Matthew Seager
with His Mother Angela

84 Cat and Dog at Duck End Farm c. 1910.
Who Wears the Apron?

85 Walking With Wolves

86 Where's Mr McGregor?

87 Akela

88 Wolf Giving Tongue

89   Llamas at Picts

90   Cattle from the
Highlands?

91   Geese from Canada?

92　One for the Pot

93　In the Spring a Young Bird's Fancy
Turns to Feathering its Own Nest

Swanning Around

95   Canada Geese in Flight

97   Crow Weather Vane

98   Aerial "Crows Nest"

99   Who's afraid of the Big Bad Scarecrow?

100   Ill-Met by Moonlight

101   Strange Goings On Amidst the Butterbur

Chapter 3   The Village Scene

This chapter, with its prospects old and new,
Features some ways in which the Village grew
And changed over the years. The Cross still stands.
Both pubs sell copious beer, of different brands;
The Village hums with busy life, and all
Dream of an extension to the Village Hall.

The Inheritance

"Time like an ever rolling stream bears all its sons away" and some of Stevington too. Until 1946, when boundary changes reduced the size of the Parish by 135 acres, the Village included the high ground to the south-west known as Picts Hill. Close by the Bedford to Northampton railway line (removed after the Beeching Report of 1962) stands Moat Farm [102], built in the 17th Century and remodelled in the early 19th Century and still a thriving working farm; however, it no longer falls within the Parish of Stevington. The old road to Picts Hill and Moat Farm started at the bottom of Wheaton Hill just beyond Duck End Farm. It is now just a track but was the main route to Turvey before the railway and the new road to the A428 were built.

In addition to territory, we have also lost some important buildings, notably the great tithe barn in Church Road, pulled down between 1872 and 1876, as well as the Hospice and Manor House nearby which were demolished at about the same time. Fortunately, much of interest has survived the ravages of time and man.

The Village is laid out in the characteristic cruciform of an Anglo-Saxon village. Descending into the Village from Wheaton Hill in the south the first building of consequence, situated on the right, is Duck End House, formerly Duck End Farm. It was a working farm until the early 1970s when the owner, David Smith, sold it. In its grounds there used to stand a charming 18th Century dovecote, all the more picturesque for its decaying fabric [107] if not for its tin roof. The dovecote had somehow escaped listing and it was demolished overnight in the early 1980s.

The next complex of buildings is the present Duck End Farm. Once there were two farms of the same name but neither owner would change the name of his. However, there the two Duck End farms stood, next to each other, albeit with a smallholding in between, and no doubt there was confusion at times. It is all the stranger as

the remaining Duck End Farm was once called "Olyffes" occupied by a family of the name of Olyffe and no one knows why the name was changed. **Plate 106** shows the garden of the present Duck End Farm as it was shortly before the Great War with the then owners, the Turney family, in the garden. Note the beehives which were a feature of many curtilages in the Village.

A striking indication of the way things change is **Plate 109**. This is the rear of the *Royal George* pub in Silver Street. The stairs seen here in the courtyard are now enclosed within the main structure and the well is filled in.

Plate 134 is a photograph of Silver Street showing a child, apparently abandoned in a pram, with a horse, probably attached to a cart, looking on. If "every picture tells a story" this should certainly give us a glimpse into the past. What exactly is the story here?

In the next picture [135], one of the oldest street views we have, a child stands outside the *Royal George*. To the right, more or less opposite the *Royal George*, there used to be a bakery (Keeper's Bakery) which along with its shop on the Silver Street frontage closed in 1973. Behind it there is now a small close of five houses called, appropriately enough, *The Bakery*. Also in the picture is a splendid sight of the striated topiary of the yew in the garden of what used to be the Village shop with the Cross in front, taken shortly after the Great War or even earlier. The yew is no longer barbered as it used to be.

Opposite the shop is a 19th Century red brick building which used to be the old Institute or Reading Room [143], built on land provided by the Tuckers of Pavenham, after whom *Tuckers Islands* in the river are named (see map in the *Village History*). The Institute was designed keep the men out of the pubs and it had a reading room to encourage sobriety. The young were given a shilling to sign the pledge which they promptly spent on beer. The Institute was closed when, to the horror of its benefactors and the Baptist Meeting which managed it, it was discovered that it had become a front for drinking and smoking.

Looking north down Church Road, directly opposite the *Red Lion* is the old off-licence advertising the availability of *Wells' Bedford Ales and Spirits* [137]. The off-licence ceased to trade around 1970 and was sold as a private house in the following year. The last licensee was Mercy Swain. The writing on the photograph indicates where Dick Ruffhead, the Village blacksmith, had his shop. Compare this with a recent photograph [138] of the same view. Further still down Church Road, looking back to the Cross, two tots pose for a picture [136] next to a cottage on the right, *Twin Cottages*, with a splendid overhanging thatch. The *Old House* on the left was formerly a dairy and a shop.

Facing back down Church Road, on the left, after the Church Rooms is the 'new' *Manor Farm House*, built by the Duke of Bedford in the early 1880s, after he demolished the old Manor House and Hospice. The *Old Vicarage*, further down on the left, dates back to the 15th Century. It was sold in 1977, a year after the last incumbent occupied it [110]. Compare this with **Plate 111**, a sketch by Bernard West drawn in 1943.

At the end of Church Road, the *Holy Well* is seen at the bottom of **Plate 114** with St Mary's church in the background. In the photograph the butterbur is discernable but not yet rampant as it is in high summer. On the right is an area that used to flood frequently and where horses were watered, though this is not very clear from the photograph. Contrast this with a watercolour wash executed by Bernard West in 1943 at the age of 16 [115] and a modern photograph [116]. Another old photograph [112] of the Church itself, surmounting the *Holy Well*, conceals the fact that the roof of the south aisle (15th Century) is ruined. The remaining shell, open to the sky, is now used for mowers and other equipment for the maintenance of the churchyard [113].

Returning to Park Road, the easterly arm of the Village, one sign of change is the view of the former Village shop, now a private house [141]. Another sign of change is reflected in a view of the road outside the *Almshouses* [125] showing Park Road circa 1900 lined with an avenue of elms and sycamores. At least seven people stand there. **Plate 127** is the same view today.

The Almshouses were founded by William Barringer. He was born in Stevington and, having made a fortune as a printer, in London left in his will of 1631 a sum of about £1600, which enabled five almshouses to be built and also funded the purchase of about 25 aces of land on the boundary between Pavenham and Felmersham to provide income for the Trust (Barringer Trust). Today that parcel of land is leased and forms part of the new Pavenham Golf Course. **Plate 129** shows the Almshouses today with four occupants standing in their doorways, from left to right: Mavis Crowe; Chris Molloy; Mary Woods; and Freda Jeffs.

Almost next door is the *Primitive Methodist Chapel* [117] which closed to worship in 1957 and was then used as a potato store. Fortunately it is now the workshop of Robert Shaftoe, organ builder, reminding us that "all art and much religion aspires to the condition of music".

To the south of Park Road lies the *Windmill*, a post mill constructed in about 1770. In 1921 Percy Keech, an undertaker, carpenter and wheelwright by trade, saw that the mill needed repair and undertook with the help of six men to do the job, which in fact he completed in a mere twelve weeks. The Mill remained in working order until 1939. In 1951 it was purchased by Bedfordshire County Council as an historic monument and was one of five contributions made by Bedfordshire to the Festival of Britain. It is now a listed building. **Plate 154** shows it as it was after Percy had restored it; **Plate 155** shows it forlorn and awaiting repair after the sails were damaged in a storm; **Plate 156** shows the repair work in progress involving much interior renewal, the restoration of the outside boarding and the replacement of the steps and tailpole. The new sails were put in place from 22 to 24 September 2004 after an absence of six years [157]. **Plates 149-53** show the work in progress.

Beyond the Windmill lies *Skylark Cottage*, a derelict reminder of the railway era in the Parish [122]. It was last occupied by Dudley Orman and his family in the 1980s. **Plate 123** shows the old railway line at Picts Hill with its splendid bridge and **Plate 124** has signs of a narrow gauge railway.

On the western arm of the Village one enters Court Lane from the Cross and at the end is a terrace of stone cottages [108]. Almost opposite, at Amen Corner, and set back from the present road is *Home Close* [128] (now called "Willow House") where the old road left the line of the modern road, continued towards the Church and then wound round to near *Meeting Farm* at West End [103]. Part of Meeting Farm dates back to the 15th Century. The former farm buildings opposite once formed part of *West End Farm* and are now converted into a private house [104]. The old farmhouse was demolished in the late 19th Century. Nearby is the *Baptist Meeting* [118] founded in 1655 and built in 1721. The last house on the left in West End is *Hart Farm* [105].)

"Change and decay in all around I see."

In the 1920s the Village was in decay, but the next decade saw a radical improvement. This leaning standpipe in Park Road [159], rusty though it be and crying out for attention, is a reminder of the days when pure drinking water was so necessary to counter disease that in 1935 the Bedford Rural District Council introduced a *"Comprehensive Scheme of Water Supply"* to all villages in the County. Altogether there are ten of these standpipes, in Park Road, Church Road, Silver Street and West End, putting an end to the use of the wells which previously were the only source of drinking water and probably polluted (see *Village History* Chapter 32 page 230).

The improvement in Stevington's living conditions was accelerated by the availability of modern transport (including the bicycle) which enabled people to work away from home and get back in reasonable time to take part in village life. Other factors, besides good water, included mains sewerage, electricity and, much later, gas. Houses which in the 1920s and 1930s were in a poor state of repair became desirable properties offering, along with all mod cons, countryside peace and the unquantifiable benefits of Village life.

Apart from the development of the closes of Farley Way, Burridge's Close and Foxbrook, there has been much infilling, extension and adaptation. The original Village School building [119] was divided into two dwellings and the old School House, occupied by the head teacher has been extended [120]. "The Barns" off Church Road, formerly part of Manor Farm, have been transformed into prestige examples of conversion [131]. Other examples in Park Road include No 58 [132]; the Old Mill House [133], much extended in recent years; and the even more recent extension of Wilf Mackness's old cottage [126], the original cottage being clearly visible to the left of the photograph. Much the same transformation was effected

much earlier to the twin house opposite.

Also in Park Road at Mill Farm stands an imposing 18th Century barn [158]. This was sold by the Duke of Bedford to the County Council as part of the Smallholdings scheme. In the early years of the 1900s it was used on a communal basis by the small-holders who hoped to survive on "three acres and a cow". The depression of the 1920s and 1930s ended those hopes. The Barn is to be converted to an alternative use in the near future, and four houses will soon be built nearby where the old pig-sties once stood.

Plate 162 should be a winning entry in some future Turner Prize Competition, featuring a crazed panel from the old farm shop [160], now sadly gone. Fortunately, a new farm shop has risen from the ashes [161].

At Park End there is another example of decay in the form of the old summerhouse by the river in the wood next to the Lawn. It was built by one of the nearby landowners and has a small harbour for a punt. Little now remains but fortunately we have a photograph from the early 1970s [121].

Pubs

In many villages the pubs are conveniently close to the church but, for historical reasons, the pubs today occupy the centre of Stevington. The *Royal George* was formed of three 18th Century cottages. The cottage next door, being rethatched in this photograph [144], shows what the *George* may have looked like once. Formerly a beer house and off-licence, it became a public house in 1911. The present *Red Lion* building dates from about 1882 and replaced an earlier public house of the same name on the site. Pub life in both the *Royal George* and the *Red Lion* (friendly rivals) feature in Chapter 5. However a clever photograph [140] manages to combine elements of both hostelries with Stevington's distinctive landmark, the Cross or Spike, between them. **Plates 145 and 146** show the *Royal George* in its Silver Street setting, old and new, while **Plate 147** pictures the *Red Lion* in floral glory commanding the Cross and the crossroads, contrasting with **Plate 148**, taken in rather different weather conditions. **Plate 142** is an inviting prospect on a wet and windy night.

103   Meeting Farm

102   Moat Farm

105   Hart Farm

104   West End Farm

106 The Garden of Duck End Farm

107 Dovecote at Duck End House as it Was

108 Jim Keech's Cottage in Court Lane

109 The *Royal George* Courtyard with the Old Well

111   The Old Vicarage in 1943: Sketch by Bernard West

110   The Old Vicarage Today

114 The Holy Well

115 Bernard West's Holy Well

116 St Mary's and the Holy Well Today

117   The Primitive Methodist Chapel Today

118   The Baptist Meeting

119   The Old Village School c. 1905

120   The Old School House Today

122 Skylark Cottage

121 Des Res. The Summerhouse in the Park Farm Wood c. 1973

123 Old Railway Bridge

124 Old Railway Line

126   Wilf Mackness's Old House

125   Park Road Looking Towards Budd's Hill and the Cross c. 1905

128   Home Close

127   The Same View Today

129   The Almshouses: *From left to right:* Mavis Crow, Chris Molloy, Mary Woods, and Freda Jeffs

130   Cottages at Park End c.1932
Bill Harris with his Father, John, and Mother, Winifred

131   John Prentice's Old Barns: What Renovation Entails

132   58 Park Road

The Old Mill House

134 Silver Street with Child in Pram

135 Silver Street with the *Royal George*

136 Church Road Yesterday Looking Towards the Cross

137 The Old Off-Licence and the Church Road Smith

138 Church Road Today

139   The Off Licence in the 1960s

140   The Two Pubs with the Cross

141   The Village Shop Decked Out for the Marriage of
The Prince of Wales

142   Last Orders at the *Lion*

143   The Institute

144 Thatching next to the *George*

145 The *Royal George* Yesterday: Oliver Cox at the Door

146 The *Royal George* Looking Towards the Cross

147   The *Red Lion* in Floral Glory

148   The *Red Lion* at Christmas

149   Rearming the Windmill: The First Cross Arm Arrives

150   The Cross Arm is Lifted into Place

151   The Bolts Go In

152   Anticipation and Expectation

153   The Second Sail Goes On

154   The Windmill in Working Order 1921

155   Dismasted and Sails Removed 1996

156   Work in Progress 2003

157   The Windmill Resailed: 24 September 2004

158   The Great Barn at Mill Farm

159   Sad Standpipe

160   The Old Farm Shop

161   The New Mill Farm Shop

162   Modern Art? The Old Mill Farm Shop

Chapter 4 Stevington at Arms

Stevingtonians rallied to the Cause
And served, some died, in both World Wars

Life in our Village would have been very different had not our lives and liberties been defended when the need arose. No book on Stevington would be complete without recording the contribution made by its sons and daughters in the defence of their country in two World Wars. In the *Village History* we included photographs of eight of the eleven soldiers who died in the Great War of 1914 - 1918. The pictures reproduced here are of some who survived both Wars.

During the First World War the much respected headmaster of Stevington School, Harry "Daddy" Read, maintained close contact by correspondence with his former pupils serving in the Armed Forces. By the end of the War he had collected together his photographs of them and written down details of their service. This material was fortunately preserved and passed by Paul Middleton to the County Archive and Records Office.

From these photographs one can see the pride with which the servicemen donned the "dress" uniforms of their respective regiments and corps and also imagine that many a mantelpiece and sideboard in the Village carried such a reminder while the servicemen were fighting in the various theatres of war.

Stevingtonians were represented in all branches of the Armed Forces, including the Women's Services and, during the Second World War, in Home Defence. Their military deployment stretched from the trenches of Flanders to the jungles of Malaya, from the deserts of North Africa to the plains of the Sudan and East Africa, and from the skies over Europe to the waters of the Atlantic. The total commitment in all theatres in the 20th Century was well over 100. Some 17 died and a number of others suffered severe physical and mental injury in the field and as prisoners of war.

163

Sgt Arthur William Bartram MM and Bar, Royal Engineers. He served in France in the Great War with the East Anglian Royal Engineers and was the most highly decorated of the Village's servicemen.

164

Able Seaman George Seamarks, Royal Navy. A member of the Royal Naval Reserve, he served in *HMS Doris* in France and Malta.

165

1st Air Mechanic Victor A Harding, Royal Flying Corps (12 Sqn RFC). He served on the Western Front 1915-18..

166

Gunner George Swain, Royal Artillery, was called up for service in 1939 but following a serious motor accident he was invalided into civilian life and served in the Home Guard.

167

Driver Walter J D Cox, Royal Army Service Corps. He served in Egypt in 1916, and later served in France with HQ Coy 60 Division Train.

168

Flt Sgt (Engineer) Rex Cox, Royal Air Force. He served in North Africa supporting the 8th Army and later in 1943 in Italy. By 1945 he had joined Transport Command, based in the Canal Zone, Egypt.

169

Bombardier Victor Ruffhead, Royal Horse Artillery. He was a regular soldier who in 1914 was serving in India.

170

Corporal James R Ruffhead, Royal Army Veterinary Corps. Volunteered for service in 1914 and served in Salonika and Egypt in 1916. He later moved to Gaza in Palestine before returning to Britain in 1919.

171

Sapper (Driver) Frank Harding, East Anglian Royal Engineers.

172

Tpr Walter Warwick. He served in the 1st Bedforshire Yeomanry.

173

Tpr William H Bowyer, The Bedfordshire Lancers. He volunteered for service in 1914 and saw action in the Middle East, taking part in the Battle of Gaza. He was twice wounded in 1917.

174

Able Seaman George J Jeffries (1897-1969). He served in the Royal Navy, 1914-18, as a stoker in *HMS Diadam* and *HMS Holy Oak*. He saw action at the battle of Jutland.

175

Sgt James Cox, The Royal Norfolk Regiment. He was severely injured and hospitalized for nearly two years 1916-17.

176

Drummer Joseph George Cowley, The Bedfordshire and Hertfordshire.Regiment. He served in Ireland, India and the Far East, and completed his career after the Second World War retiring with the rank of Major.

177

Sgt Arthur Stanbridge enlisted in The East Surrey Regiment in 1917 and served in Flanders, where he was slightly gassed, and later in Germany. In 1919 he volunteered for operations to aid the White Russians.

178

Signalman Sydney C Glidle 2/5th Bn The Bedfordshire Regiment. Served in France in 1916 when he was captured and remained a prisoner of war until 1918.

179

Pte Philip Cox, 3rd Bn The Bedfordshire Regiment. Served in Egypt and later in India in 1916.

180

(left) Pte Frank W Hulett, 1st Bn The Bedfordshire Regiment. Served in Egypt in 1916. *(right)* L Cpl Fred G (Ted) Hulett, Provost Corps 68 Provost Bn. He served in France in 1916 and was captured and held as a prisoner of war.

163　Sgt Arthur
William Bartram

164　Able Seaman
George Seamarks

165　1st Air
Mechanic Victor
A Harding

166　Gunn
Georg
Swai

167　Driver
Walter J D Cox

168　Flt Sgt
(Engineer) Rex Cox

169　Bombardier
Victor Ruffhead

170　Corporal
James R
Ruffhead

171　Sapper (Driver)
Frank Harding

172　Tpr Walter
Warwick

173　Tpr William
H Bowyer

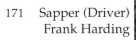

174　Able Seaman
George J Jeffries

175   Sgt James Cox

176   Drummer Joseph
George Cowley

177   Sgt Arthur
Stanbridge

178   Signalman Sydney C Glid

179   Private Philip Cox

180   Private Frank W Hulett and
L Cpl Fred G (Ted) Hulett

Chapter 5   The Village in Action

In all the various disciplines of Sport
Inter-village battles have been fought
At football, cricket, tennis even darts.
Villagers accomplished in the Social Arts,
Revel, feast, combine and sing in choirs
And variously fulfil their hearts' desires.
To know about the goings-on there've been
You only have to read the Village Magazine.

Stevington has always been the sort of village where folk seize every opportunity to come together to enjoy themselves. The pubs and sports clubs have always provided the ideal rendezvous.

Pubs

In the good old days Stevington boasted at least four pubs, but today it is left to the *Royal George* and *Red Lion* to welcome us and keep us supplied. The *Royal George* retains its original cosy, low oak beam charm. The current landlord is Gary Harber **[185]** who has a reputation for traditional cooking, and a Tuesday dining club meets to enjoy it regularly **[189]**. The pub attracts many visitors and a recent visit by the French Resistance *Michelles* can be seen in **Plate 203**, while some of the regulars tend to get into the habit **[204]**. Festivals are observed here and a photograph taken from the front door shows Richard Galley standing in Silver Street piping in the New Year **[197]**. The pub hosts many competitive sporting activities including pool, darts and even golf, and for many a year has fielded successful quiz teams.

The *Red Lion*, overlooking the Cross, is the oldest watering hole in the Village (though rebuilt in the 1880s on the site of the earlier alehouse), and with its larger gardens attracts the outdoor type, in summer at least **[194]**. Geoff and Karen Gallimore **[186]**, as landlord and landlady until May 2004, continued the tradition of having live music about the place. **Plate 188** is of the new landlords, Jim Wannerton and Jodie Hague, seen here with Jeanette Wannerton **Plate 200** shows the outside of the *Red Lion* some 50 years or so ago with an interesting trio who look as though they are set to enthral, while **Plate 199** shows Pete Bonas with his brother Paul Bonas (formerly of Silver Street), serenading their audience in more recent times **[201]**. Also, being close to the Cross, the *Lion* has long been a favoured venue of the Bedford

Morris who regularly dance outside and drink within **[195 and 196]**.

Plates 184 and 187 are rare shots of Thomas Burridge who married Martha Field (nee Ruffhead), the first licensee of the rebuilt *Red Lion*. She also owned the brickworks next to the house now called *Tankards* on the Pavenham Road. Burridge kept the *Lion* from 1903-46. His wife had held the licence from 1891-1903.

The *Red Lion* has its fair share of regulars, and the three with the prettiest legs can be seen enjoying a pint in the bar **[190]** though they cannot compete in pulchritude with the friendly staff **[202]**. The pub supports a good number of pub games and **Plate 191** shows the local Women's Institute darts team who seem to be 3:1 up against their opponents.

Some former publicans got on so well with their customers that they settled in the Village. Jennifer and Graham Bentham kept the *George* from 1988 to 1992 **[183]**; Pam Luck (see **189**) followed the Benthams. Peter and Sue Bishop kept the *Lion* from 1977-86 **[182]**; and Anne and Brian Westbrook followed them from 1992-4 **[181]**.

Sport

Until fairly recent years Stevington's sporting life centred on outdoor pursuits, especially football and cricket. Both have had a following in the Village for so long that just which one came first is lost in the mists of time. However, it is known that both have been played for well over a century, and certainly by 1901 both had established clubs and were competing with teams from neighbouring villages. Like all clubs their fortunes waxed and waned with some notable successes and defeats.

Plate 209 is the oldest photograph of the *Stevington Football Team* taken early in the 20th Century. The two players we have identified are

Alan Cox's uncle, Phil Cox, and Billy Field. **Plates 210, 211 and 212** are of the Stevington football teams of the 1950s and portray some dedicated club members. Most tasted victory when the teams won the divisional championships in the late 1940s and early 1950s. The Village currently has two football teams playing respectively in the Bedford and District League (Premier Division) and in Associate Division One. **Plates 213 and 214** show the first XI in action, including long-established players such as Gareth and Darren King. They are coached by Roger Easingwood **[216]** and encouraged and supported by Dennis King **[215]** who has tended the playing field with loving care for many years. There is also a band of keen youngsters who pursue the sport and use the five-a-side facilities at the playing field **[217]**.

The *Stevington Cricket XI* plays in the Bedford and District Leagues and **Plates 223 and 224** show them in action. **Plate 225** is of the supporters' club; Lucy King keeps a spare ball in case of the odd "over the hedge" sixer. Earlier teams are shown in **Plates 218 and 219** and these include some of the Village's celebrated sportsmen. One of the more unusual matches to take place on the playing field occurred in 1977 during the Queen's Jubilee celebrations. The ladies of the Village challenged the men, the twist being that the men, playing left-handed, had to dress as women and *vice versa*. All rose to the occasion with a spectacular catch being made by the late Brian Hopkinson (former landlord of the *Royal George*) in his handbag. **Plates 221 and 222** show the teams, but just who played for whom and what the final score was remains a mystery to all concerned, not least the spectators.

The cricket and football teams have traditionally drawn on the same pool of enthusiasts. George Curtis, holding the ball in **Plate 212**, was one of those who excelled at both the summer and the winter game.

The *Social Centre* acts as the hub for many Village activities and one of the "new" sports that has gained in popularity and takes place there is carpet bowls. The Club was formed by a group of enthusiasts in 1990 spearheaded by Mick Haggerwood. Within a few years of its formation, the Club won the Knock-Out Championship in Luton and continues to compete in the local leagues **[226-228]**. Stan Walker's son and grandson have both followed in his bowling footsteps, and **Plate 236** shows the three of them in their club strip.

During the 1920s and 1930s a Tennis Club thrived in the Village **[233]**, playing on the court at Marion Field's house. Nowadays it is table tennis that is proving more popular, with five teams currently enjoying success in the Bedford and District League. **Plates 229 and 230** show the action and the concentration. **Plate 231** shows Clive Rudd, Norman Beesley, and Malcolm Nightingale, founder members of the Stevington Club, while **Plate 232** shows Roger Day and Richard Blayney celebrating their victory in the Milton Keynes Summer League in 2002.

A regular event at the Village fete used to be a tug of war match and **Plate 240** shows a winning combination that included Charlie Finch and Chris Boniface.

Bedford Sailing Club, founded in 1954, is also an integral part of the Village sporting scene, having attracted many dinghy sailors and families over the years to its beautiful location by the river. **Plate 268** shows young beginners enjoying their first sailing experience. Some of those who learnt the ropes at the Sailing Club have gone on to ocean sailing. The Club's compound is a sought-after venue for barbecues **[275]**, birthday celebrations and even wedding receptions. In **Plate 274** two Club stalwarts guard the beer at the Summer Barbecue while things happen on the water **[270-72]**. Chris Boniface **[479]** ensures that this beautiful spot always looks good. The present Commodore is Lynn Christison (see **325**). Other recent Commodores include Peter Francis **[239]**, Peter Hart (see **410**) and Fiona Frossell.

In 1983 Charlie Homer **[261]** instigated the first Stevington 7.5 mile road race. It is held each May and continues to attract many runners, young and old, from all over the country. **Plate 247** shows George Strong starting one of the first runs, while **Plate 248**, taken just a few years ago, shows the start from outside the Village Hall. **Plate 249** shows the new "fast start" technique currently being used by the Stevington youngsters. Getting to the finish line is a real achievement and **Plates 250-257** show just how hard it gets. The reception and medal awarded by our Brownie troop **[258]** is very welcome indeed.

Bill Harris of Court Lane was a talented runner in his time. He competed in cross-country for the County and for British Rail and was Bedford Athletic Club champion in the late

1950s at cross country, road and track over distances of two to 15 miles **[259 and 260]**. Cycling to work at Bedford Station kept him fit. David Stanbridge was also quick out of the blocks in his day **[245]**.

Mike Grafton, who played football and cricket for Stevington, as well as football in the Isthmian League and cricket at county league level, instigated and organized the Stevington Ski Trips in the 1980s and 1990s **[242]**. The first, at Serre Chevalier, included over 50 Villagers aged six to 60. Mike is pictured here with his wife, Angie **[241]**, who played squash at County level. Anne Seaton **[235]** played tennis for the County and still plays at that level as a veteran. In 1984 the Village ladies were champions in the Inter Village Sports **[234]**. Rosemary Stanbridge **[237]** played netball for Northants and hockey for Bedfordshire. Natalie Ward played rounders at a national level **[265]** and her sister, Stephanie, competed in gymnastics at the same level.

Village sporting achievements cover a wide range of activities and there have been many successful individuals including the late Brian "Bumble" Stapleton and Peter Jackson **[238]**, both of whom played for Bedford RUFC ("The Blues"). Peter also represented the East Midlands. "Titch" Haynes, who lived in Farley Way in the 1970s, was a celebrated Blues player and regularly represented the East Midlands; he was later President of the Club.

Indeed, Stevington abounds in sporting talent. For example, Jane Poulter **[243]** was an international oarswoman. Some Village residents of the past have been international celebrities such as Diane Leather, the former women's one mile world record holder, and more recently the Olympic oarsman, Graham Smith, lately of Duck End House. Paula Radcliffe was a frequent if fleeting visitor as she pounded through the North Bedfordshire lanes in training.

Riding has a keen following in the Village and some youngsters have excelled at an international level: Harriet Cole represented Great Britain as a junior **[262]**. Nick Finch **[263]** and Charlotte Finch **[264]** represented Oakley Hunt West in tetrathlon competitions at a national level. Swimming and deep sea diving have also enjoyed popularity, but one of the rarest pursuits must be kite bugging, practised by Mike Bush and his sons **[266]**.

An exponent of something entirely different is

Stuart Robinson who held the world model powerboat record and was president of the sport's governing body for some years **[267]**. James Petre's pursuit is also somewhat out of the ordinary **[244]**. He climbs the "Munros", the significant Scottish peaks, and has conquered over half of the 284 odd total.

However, fishing attracts the greatest numbers and can be fiercely competitive. Even so, it has its more relaxing moments. The lads are tying flies in the *Red Lion* in anticipation of the next catch and in mellow mood reminiscing over the size of the last (see **207**). John Duffield (far right) has captained an England team against Scotland in a fly-fishing competition. On the other hand Rob Puckett does not have to dream; he has actually caught something (see Chapter 7 **475**).

Cycling has been an active pastime for some time with the Ouse Valley offering many challenges. **Plates 276 and 277** show some cyclists enjoying a ride through the Village, while in Plate **279** Roger Seaton's battery seems to have run out. Not so Marion Field's **[287]**. Most, it appears, prefer not to be self-propelled **[281-286]**, although Gill King seems to be less nervous about travelling solo **[280]**. For others, who enjoy Stevington's network of footpaths, Shanks' pony is good enough **[330]**. And there's always the scooter **[299]**.

Leisure

It should not be imagined for one moment that all Village activity is concentrated in the pubs or even on the playing field. Until the late 19th Century most social activity revolved around the three churches. The advent of the bicycle and the internal combustion engine radically affected mobility and the motorised charabanc, previously horse-drawn **[289]**, brought the "outing" into being **[294]**. **Plates 292 and 293** show the "Bluebird" with and without its hood. Sunday afternoon trips to Turvey for tea were a regular occurrence. The modern version of the charabanc is seen here in the form of David Litchfield's coach **[295]**.

Other modes of transport were used to get to work. The chain ferry in Boat Meadow ferried labourers to the Oakley side to work at Westfield Farm **[291]**, though in this picture not much work is being done.

The harvest supper has always been popular and is traditionally held in the Church Rooms

[318-319] and **Plate 320** depicts the auction of harvest vegetables. The Christmas Concert in the Village Hall has also been a well-attended and amusing event for several decades [321-6].

The Silver Jubilee in 1977 saw the Village *en fete* and **Plate 302** shows George Strong opening the Jubilee fete at the playing field when every child received a Jubilee mug. The youngest, Isobel Hart, was six weeks old.

For a number of years the Stevington Guy Fawkes' night was a very popular event [312-317]. Regretfully, stringent health and safety regulations and crippling insurance costs mean that it was last held in 2002.

The Village Hall has witnessed many thespian occasions. There was a theatre group between the Wars, and after the last War there was a new impetus with the production by the Social Centre of *Cinderella* in 1988 [327]. Since then there have been innumerable shows, conducted under the auspices of the Social Centre, the Sailing Club and others. **Plate 331** shows the girls on form and the impresario himself, Rob Puckett, directing in **Plate 328** and performing in **Plate 335. Plate 332** portrays a monstrous regiment of Stevington evacuees in the production *Careless Talk* as well as Charlie Finch on song [333]. The most recent production was of Willie Rushton's *Our Day Out* [329 and 330]. The Village Hall is also a popular venue for parties, wedding receptions, and many other social events [301, 303, 304 and 336-346].

But when all is said and done, many of us simply like to sit and see the world go by [297], and this is not an activity confined to the more mature Villagers [306 and 308].

181 Anne and Brian Westbrook

182 Sue and Peter Bishop

183 Jennifer and Graham Bentham

184 Thomas Burridge outside the *Lion*

185   Gary Harber, Landlord of the *Royal George*

186   Geoff and Karen Gallimore

187   Thomas Burridge with a Special Barrel

188   Jodie Hague, Jeanette and James Wannerton

189   The Tuesday Dining Club
Barbara Collins, Avis Clayton, Franie Hodgkinson, Pam Luck and Delia Lee

190   Anything but Legless: Seaton, Hart and Garrett

The WI Darts Team

192   The *Royal George*
       Pool Team

193   *Royal George* Regulars
       Winning the Rugby
       World Cup 2003

194　The *Red Lion* Garden

195　Morris Men Performing at the Cross

196   Morris Accordian and Squeeze Box

197   The Phantom Piper; Richard Galley

198   The Snarling Beasties

199   Pete and Paul Bonas

200   Wandering Minstrels Outside the *Red Lion*

201   A *Red Lion* Audience

202   Service with a Smile

203   French Resistance *Michelles*
Chrissie Fitch, Jane Thomas, Linda Penney, Anne Westbrook, Jackie Ward and Sue Smith

204   Getting into the Habit; en route to the *Royal George*

205   Non-Alcoholic Dominoes at the Church Rooms c. 1935

206   Domino Theory at the *Red Lion*

207   Anglers Adjusting Their Flies
David Rhodes, Mickey Garrett, Michael Robinson and John Duffield

208   Death of Conversation: Three Down
Jean Blayney, Richard Blayney and Ray Cox

209   The Stevington Football Team c. 1900
Phil Cox (*Front Row, Second Left*), Billy Field (*Front Row Far Right*)

210   Stevington Football XI Bedfordshire League Division 1 Winners 1956-7
Back Row: A Cox (Hon Sec and Treasurer), J White (Linesman)R Munns, A Woolston, J Sheehan, J Gibbons, P Gurney, A
Woods, A Clark, Col J B Smith (President) L Aspley (Trainer)
Front Row: C Bird, D Mackness, R Hammond, L Myers (Captain), H Barnes, J Warman, A Stone

211   Stevington Football Club Division I Winners 1953-4

Back Row: A Cox (Secretary and Treasurer), L Aspley (Linesman) W Bird (Vice-Captain), D Mackness, A Sharp, J Gibbons, J Chambers G Rainbow (Trainer), J Cowley (Chairman)

Centre Row: R Seamarks, C Blackwood, G Curtis (Captain) C Bird, N Peach

Front Row: B Prigmore, W Lee

212   Stevington Football Club Bedfordshire League Champions Division II 1949-50

nding: J Cowley (Chairman) J Chambers, J Quinney, L Aspley, P Pell, B Everest, B Cox, A Cox (Secretary) R Warwick (Trainer)

Sitting: R Seamarks, L Cook, W Bird, C Bird (Captain), G Curtis, E Toms, J Keech, Simon Hall

213   The First XI in Action

214   The Modern Football XI
Back Row: Gareth King, Duncan Young, Nick Fernandez, Darren Pritchard, Steve Ballister,
Gavin White, James Mackay, Andrew Sly, Mark George, Roger Easingwood (Coach)
*Front Row:*Neil Woolerton, Stephen Watts, Tony Stanton, David Milkovic, Tony Riley

215 Dennis King

216 Roger Easingwood

217 Five-a-side
Back row: Danny Kular, Tom Strutt, Laurence Bentham, Joe Strutt
Front Row: Rory Petre, Sarah Rock, David Wood

218   Stevington Cricket XI
Back Row: Nigel Chadburn, Jeff Comb, Graham Bentham, Norman Beesley, Gareth King, Mike Grafton
Front Row: Richard Ellis, Paul Parkin, Willy Stanbridge, Shane King, Darren King

219   Stevington Cricket XI
Back Row: Steve Jeffries, Maurice Day, Robert Albery, Paul Hodgkinson, Dave Humber, Mel Cox, Billy Saunders, Bill Jowe
Front Row: David Mackness, Wally Neale, Graham Cox, Brian Bushby

220   Junior Cricket

*Back Row:*Ed Osborne,?, Ollie Thompson, Norman Beesley, Edward Puffett, Sylvia Beesley, Fee Thompson

Front Row:?, Andrew Grafton, Willy Stanbridge, James Grafton, Damian Pell, James Warburton

221   Stevington Ladies' XI

Back Row: Jim Crowe, Peter Keech, Mick Woods, David Litchfield, Dennis King, ?, Ken Wagstaff, Bernard Cox, Brian Hopkinson

Front Row: Stan Walker, ?, Mel Cox

222   Stevington Gentlemens' XI

From Left to Right: Gill King, Shirley Dickinson, Jacqui Ward, Rosemary Stanbridge, Di Bailey, Ruth Winfield, Janet Litchfield, Jean Lockwood,Carol Woods, Clare Stapleton, Marion Watkins

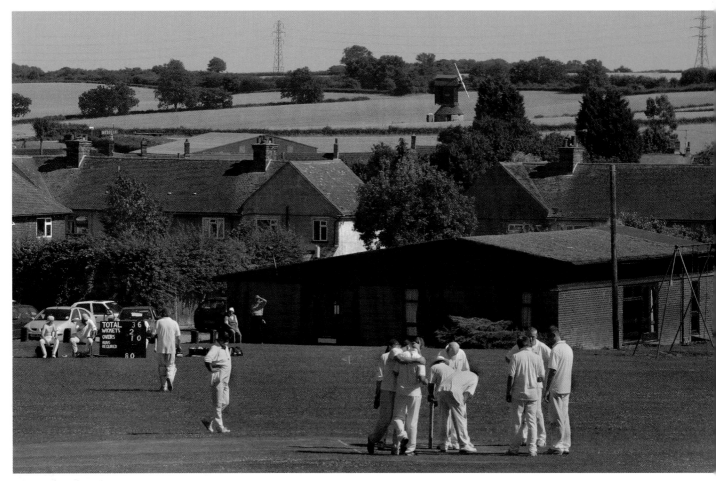

223   Stevington Cricket XI in Action

224   Stevington Cricket XI in the Field

225 Supporter's Club: Lucy King

226   Carpet Bowls in Actio

227   The Vicar Appeals
       to the Almighty

228   Just Bowling Along

229   Table Tennis in Action

230   Junior Table Tennis

232   Roger Day and Richard Blayney

231   Clive Rudd, Norman Beesley and Malcolm Nightingale

233   Stevington Tennis Club c 1936
Back Row: Harry Warwick,?, Mr Tucker, Sybil Field
Middle Row: ?, Eileen Quick,? Sue Cox, George Cox
Front Row: Marion Field, George Coleman, Audrey Field, Joe Tandy

234   Inter-Village Sports
Back Row: Elaine Mustoe, Johanna Whitney,
Angie Grafton, Judith Cummings
Front Row: Carol Pyner, Stephanie Field, Kay Nichol

235   Anne Seaton

236   The Walkers: Michael Stan and Graham

237   Rosemary Stanbridge

238   Brian "Bumble" Stapleton and Peter Jackson

Peter Francis, Sailing Club Commodore in the
1980s Splicing the Mainbrace

240   Tug O'War

241   Angie and Mike Grafton

242   *Stevington on Ice*

243   Jane Poulter Dipping Her Oars In

244   James Petre in Peak Condition

245 David Stanbridge

246 Countdown

247 George Strong Fires the Starting Pistol

248 Start of the Stevington Run

249 Fast Start Technique: Tom Strutt, Greg Stephenson, Sarah Rock and Joe Strutt

256 Sue Thornton

257 Andy Stupple

258 Brownies Come to the Rescue

259   Bill Harris Receiving Yet
Another Trophy

260   Bill Harris (right) with Ron Clark

261   Charlie Homer

262   Harriet Cole

263   Nick Finch on Buddy

264   Charlotte Finch on Garvey

265 Natalie Ward

266 Mike and Peter Bush

267 Stuart Robinson up to his Knees in It

268 The Oppies
en Masse

269 Toppers: Kim Seaton
Leading Tom Hart

270   Come in No 1
Your Time Is Up

271   Down by the Riverside

272   Warburton Triplets
Coming into Port

273   The Fly-Fishing Lesson

4   Iain Morrison and Roger
Penney Guarding the Beer

275   Sailing Club
Summer Barbecue

276   In Tandem

277   Safety First

278   Tony Hollins

279   Power Assisted Roger Seaton

280　Uphill Struggle: Gill King

281　Black Leather Convoy

282 Rex Cox on his BSA

285   Stevington's Hell's Angels

287   Marion Field Outstrips Them All

286   Junior Leathers: Tom Barrett, Samantha Prentice, Oliver Barrett

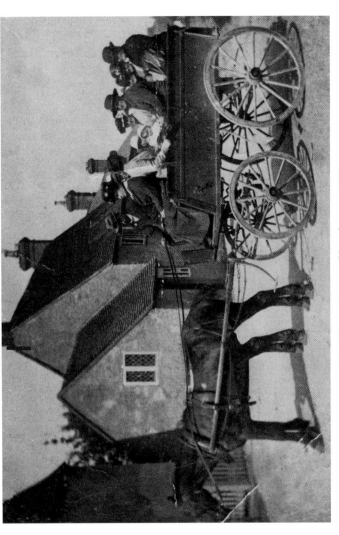

289 Horse-Drawn Charabanc c. 1910

291 The Chain Ferry across the Ouse in Boat Meadow

288 Pony and Trap at Hart Farm c. 1890

290 Harry Field's Lorry c. 1934

293 Bluebird on a Fine Day

295 David Litchfield Coaches

292 Bluebird with Tonneau

294 The Excursion

297   Chewing the Fat: Ken Prentice, Jim Swain and Harry Pearson

296   Swinging Along

301 Partying at the Village Hall

304 Craft Fair and Football Match Framed by the Village Hall Window

302 George Strong Opening the 1977 Jubilee Fete

303 Wedding Reception at the Village Hall: Jean and Richard Blayney

305　Flood at the Top of Silver Street August 1980

306　Last Sitting at the Cross

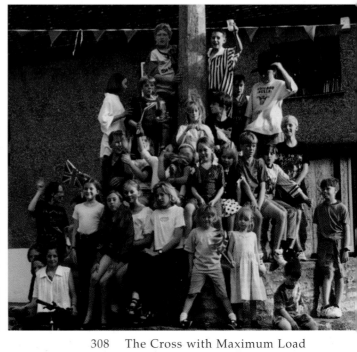

307　Rub-a-Dub-Dub, Six Scamps in a Tub

308　The Cross with Maximum Load

309   Jubilee Fancy
      Dress 1935

310   Coronation Fancy Dress 1953

311   Jubilee 2002

318   Harvest Supper Toast

319   Harvest Supper By Candlelight

320   Auction of Harvest Vegetables

321 Christmas Concert:
    Male Voice Choir
    From Left to Right: Bob Eadie,
    Andy Smith, John Strutt,
    Roy Pryn, Dave Fitch,
    David Warburton, Bob Hart
    and Ken Manning

322 Concentration: Evie
    McManus and Joan Hart

323 Peter Stileman
    Compering the Show

324   Philip Bond Tickling the Ivories

325   The Orchestra
Back Row: Liz Cox, Isobel Perl, Charlotte
Campion, Evie McManus,
Front Row: Jackie Gooding, Suzy Penney, Tom
McVey, Alex McxManus, Lynn Christison

326   Interval Scrummage

327 *Cinderella*

328 The Director (Rob Puckett) Giving the Cast a Dressing Down

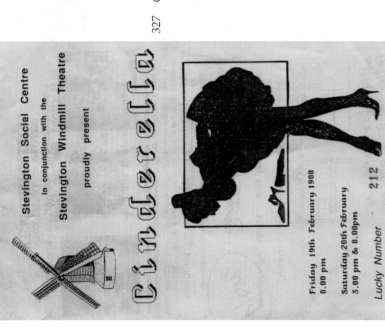

331 *Careless Talk*: The Girls in Action

332 *Careless Talk* Evacuees

334 Dave Fitch

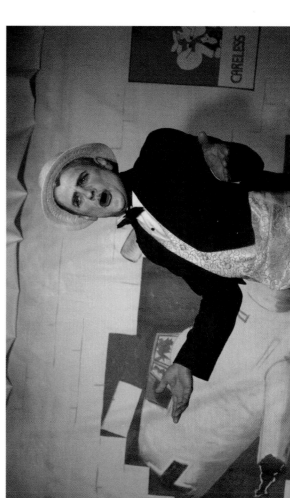

333 Charlie Finch On Song

335 The Director Himself:
Rob Puckett in *Careless Talk*

336　The Bonas Brothers in Consort

337　The Snarling Beasties in Shadow

345-350 Conversazioni

351   Betty Bishop and Barbara Collins see the Joke

352   Uncle's Wisdom Imparted: Mick Garrett and Sarah Rock

Chapter 6   *Making It Happen*

Religion generates amazing power;
Saxon Villagers put up St Mary's tower,
And Bunyan, fired with religious zest
Inspired dissenting Baptists to protest
Against Church law and build their Meeting here
In Stevington. Our Parish Council too
Shrewdly applies its slender revenue;
And in the early pages if you look
You'll see it wisely underwrote this book.

A significant number of Villagers give up many hours of their time to making organisations function and flourish.

Governance

Stevington's first local councillors were returned under the Local Government Act 1888. Until 1974 Stevington was part of Bedford Rural District Council. The first councillor of note of whom we have a photograph is Percy Keech [353]. He was a wheelwright, carpenter and undertaker who restored the Windmill after the First World War. He was responsible for bringing foul water drainage to the Village in 1936.

The last Stevington councillor to represent the Village on the RDC before it was abolished on 31 March 1974 was Paul Hodgkinson [357]. He did much useful work for the Village while on the Council and afterwards, as he was a keen supporter of the football and cricket clubs and also choirmaster at St Mary's. He was an accomplished pianist and often played the organ in church. When the Church was heated by solid fuel Paul stoked the boiler and the crunch of coke underfoot at Evensong was a sure indication that he had been there. His untimely death in 1995 robbed the Village of an undoubted character.

Jim Brandon of Carlton has represented Stevington as an Independent on the Bedford Borough Council since 1983 (see 363). At County level, the first councillor elected after reorganisation in 1974 was Dr Mike Kelly. He was succeeded by Phyllis Gershon of Harrold who still represents the Village (see 363).

The Parish Council as a civil parish council first met in 1894. Two former parish councillors of long-standing who served the Council post-war are pictured in Chapter 7: Marion Field (see

Chapter 7 470) and Ken Prentice, seen here with his family (see Chapter 7 480) and in **Plate 354** on parade. Ken's cousin, John Prentice, who farmed at Manor Farm, was also active on the Parish Council. Another long-serving councillor was Alan Cox (see *Village History* page 111). He has been an elder of the Baptist Meeting for over fifty years and was Secretary of the Football Club from 1934 until Dennis King took over some thirty years ago.

David Stanbridge [361] connects their era with the present day. A farmer, born in Stevington at Duck End Farm, he has served on the Parish Council since 1970 and was chairman from 1970 to 1981. He is also chairman of the Stevington Historical Trust and a trustee of the Barringer Trust.

The present Parish Council is chaired by Doreen Pendlington [358]. A former teacher, she has been Chairman since 1998. She is seen here with the 2004 Parish Council [363]. The other occupants of the chair since David Stanbridge stood down were Paul Middleton (1981-85) [359], Ken Davies (1985-91) [360], and John Ward (1991-98) [362].

Religion

There were three churches in Stevington until comparatively recent times: St Mary's, the Baptist Chapel and the Primitive Methodist Chapel. The "Prims" closed in 1957 but took on a new lease of life as the workshop of Robert Shaftoe, organ builder [386]. The buildings are illustrated in Chapter 3.

St Mary's

The earliest picture we have of any Stevington clergyman is that of the then vicar, Rev J R H Duke, officiating at the laying of the foundation stone of the Church Rooms in 1897 (see *Village History* page 99). He was vicar when a dispute arose over the use of the Church Rooms which led to a certain coolness between Anglicans and Non-Conformists which fortunately has been healed in recent times. **Plate 365** shows Canon Arthur Sproule officiating in 1927 at the dedication of the War Memorial.

Of the post-War incumbents, Rev Donald Macrory **[366]**, a learned Ulsterman, is still remembered with affection by many. He was a mild-mannered, even shy, man whose pastoral care was outstanding. He was vicar from 1968 until 1976 and was the last incumbent to live in the Vicarage. Father Lawrence MacDonald was priest in charge from 1999 to 2003 (see Chapter 5 **227 and 320**). His successor, Rev David Hunter **[368]**, is from New Zealand.

St Mary's has been well-served over the years by some exceptional church wardens. The late Eddie Clayton, pictured here with his fellow churchwarden at the time, Ken Ward, and Rev Geoffrey Cowley **[367]**, is reputed to have regularly rung three of the Church bells unaided.

Marina and Albert Markham have long been active in church affairs and have held churchwarden posts at different times (see Chapter 7 **468**). The current churchwarden is Jean Lockwood (see **364**).

The bells fell silent from 1978 because the cradle was dangerous. With some crucial assistance from Tony Hollins, a metallurgist and foundryman of Farley Way (see Chapter 5 **278**), the bells rang out again in 1991. **Plates 387 and 388** show the strengthening of the Anglo-Saxon tower in progress, while **Plates 389 and 390** show the operation of re-hanging the bells. Meanwhile, the old tower team had melted away and the task of training a new team fell to Patrick Albon, formerly of Park Road.

The first tower captain of the new team was David Gorham of Burridge's Close **[391]**. The current tower captain is Rosemary Maclaine seen below with current members of the team **[392]**.

St Mary's has had number of regular organists in recent times. Ann Warburton is pictured in **Plate 395**. Until recently she coached and conducted the choir which is convened on an *ad hoc* basis, principally for the Christmas Festival of Nine Lessons and Carols **[393]** and the Village Hall concert. She has passed the baton to Philip

Bond. **Plate 397** is of Josie Hunter who was an organist for many years. Philip Bond also plays the organ in Church from time to time (see Chapter 5 **324**).

Ralph Jeffries of Silver Street built the Church pulpit and also made the Church gates **[394 and 396]**. He learnt his joinery at J P White's in Bedford and then worked for many years at the Royal Aeronautical Establishment at Thurleigh.

The Parochial Church Council was established in its current form in 1894 when the civil Parish Council separated from the Vestry. The current PCC is pictured below **[364]**.

A goodly number of weddings, baptisms and funerals are held at St Mary's each year, as they are at the Baptist Meeting. A few of the happier occasions are illustrated below **[369, 370, 373 and 374]** and one of the recent sad occasions **[371 and 372]**. One popular event in the Church calendar is the Christingle service for children held during Advent **[375 and 376]**.

The Baptist Meeting

The Baptist Meeting continues to play a full part in Village life. However, photographs of former pastors are rare and we are fortunate to have one of Rev James H Brooksbank (1928-30) seen here with his wife **[377]**. Trevor Ogden, who came to Stevington from Bromham, is the current pastor. **Plates 378-9** show him taking the service with a congregation while **Plate 380** reveals the font ready for baptismal immersion. In the early years of the Meeting baptism was carried out in a baptismal pool at the river bank. This "special place", probably Woodcraft **[384]**, was still being used after the construction of the baptistery in the Church Yard around 1835.

The School

The School, which opened in 1864 (see Chapter 3 **119**), was first attended by 62 children from the age of three. Sixty years later the roll included some 129 names. One outstanding headmaster, Harry "Daddy" Read (1894 - 1918), ruled with a rod of iron for 24 years, but he had a great affection for his former pupils and wrote innumerable letters to those serving abroad in the First World War. He is seen in **Plate 401** with his wife, Helen (nee Smith), of Duck End **[400]**.

Over the years the School achieved notable successes and raised educational standards. Sadly, in 1983, as part of a re-organization of educational policy in Bedfordshire, the School was closed and is now converted into two houses. The last teacher to live in the School House (see Chapter 3 **120**) was Mrs Marion Watkins (nee Tysoe) **[408]**. Some earlier School photographs are reproduced at **Plates 402-4**.

Trusts

The oldest Village trust is the Barringer Trust established in 1631. It manages its five Almshouses and also owns valuable land in Pavenham (see Chapter 3 **129**). The current chairman is Albert Markham and the other trustees are Aileen English, Reg Bishop, David Stanbridge, Rev Lawrence McDonald and Rev David Hunter.

A more recent Village trust is the Stevington Historical Trust which produced this book and the preceding volume *Stevington: The Village History*. It grew out of an informal group which started to meet, irregularly, in the 1970s and organised exhibitions from time to time. The Trust was formed initially to produce the *Village History*. The current trustees are seen in **Plate 410**. The object of the Trust is to research and popularise the history of Stevington. Its sister group, the Friends, was formed to further this aim. The chairman of the Friends is Peter Conquest, seen here in his 16th Century bishop's robes in which he officiates with the Sealed Knot **[411]**. He was Lord-General of the Sealed Knot Royalist Armie from 1986 to 1994. **Plate 412** shows him lecturing on Stevington's role in the Civil War, appropriately attired, with a Sealed Knot colleague, musketeer Simon Rockwood. **Plate 413** depicts Stuart Antrobus lecturing to the Friends on the Windmill in 2003.

Committees

The Social Centre and Village Hall Committee was first established soon after the Second World War and aims to be representative of all leisure interests in the Village. The late Arthur Bowman was Chairman when the present Village Hall was completed, and Bill Wills-Moren, the then Keeper of the House and Grounds, was responsible for receiving it from the contractors in 1974.

Gary Thomas is the current chairman, and the Committee **[415]** is engaged in a concerted effort

to raise funds for a sizeable extension to the Village Hall. Recent chairwomen of the Committee include Ged Puckett (see Chapter 7 **463**) and Anne Westbrook (see Chapter 5 **181**).
.
The Women's Institute is another association of long standing in the Village. It was founded in 1943 by Dorothy "Cherry" Robinson **[356]**, the first chairwoman and wife of George Robinson **[355]** of Hart Farm. She occupied the chair until 1972 and also served as a Justice of the Peace. The branch **[414]** currently has a membership of 24 and the chairwoman is Pam Rolls. They also have a much-feared darts team (see Chapter 5 **191**).

353   Percy Keech with his Son, Jim

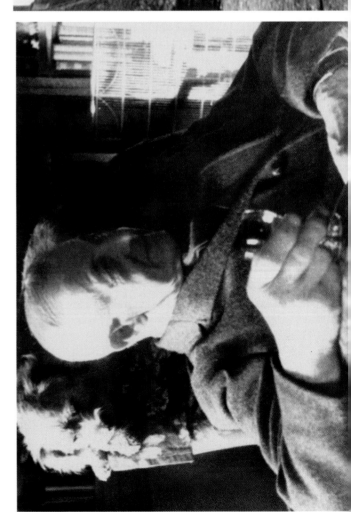

354   Ken Prentice as Jorrocks with his Admirers

359
Paul
Middleton

362
John
Ward

358
Doreen
Pendlington

361
David
Stambridge

357
Paul
Hodgkinson

360
Ken Davies

363   The Parish Council
From left to right: Doreen Pendlington (Chairman), Barbara Davies (Clerk), Sandra Proud, Brian Westbrook, Jacqui Ward, Ji[...] Brandon, Phyllis Gershon, Alison Campion, Bob Poulter, David Stanbridge

364   The Parochial Church Council
Back Row: Tom Benson, Margaret Benson, Bob Hart, Jean Lockwood
Middle Row: Tricia Lennie, Avis Clayton, Marina Markham, Margaret Jackson, Clare Stapleton
Front Row: Frances Hirst, Roy Pryn, Rev David Hunter, Sally Macdonald, Patricia Gillam

365 Canon Sproule: War Memorial Dedication 1927

367 Eddie Clayton, Rev Geoff Cowley and Ken Ward

366 Reverend Donald Macrory
in Retirement on Pilgrimage by the Sea of Galilee

368 Rev David Hunter

369 Nuptials of Ron and Denise Randall

370   Flower Festival Displays

373   Flower Festival Concert:: Trish Gillam on "Husbandry"

374   Flower Festival Concert: Jane O'Connor and Tom Benson

375   Christingle Service

376   Lighting the Candles

378   Service with the Commemorative Stained Glass Window

377
Rev James
and Mrs
Brooksbank

382
The Wedding
of Lillian and
Jim Swain

383
The Wedding of Eric
Cox and Lily Organ
From left to right:
Eric Cox, Lily Organ,
Don Cox, Vivienne Cox,
Bert Organ, Mona Cox

385
Jim Swain's Stags

381   Dedication of the Stained Glass Window at the Baptist Meeting 14 March 1948
Front Row: Paul Field, Charley Field, Alan Cox, Rev Whittle,
George Warwick, Mr T C Skeffington-Lodge MP, Keith Laslett

384   The "Special Place"

386   Robert Shaftoe's Workshop

387   Support for the Belfry

388   Strengthening the Belfry

389   Preparing the Bell

390   Elevation of the Bell

391   Tower Captain David Gorham and the Bellringers: Jean Edwards, David Gorham, Terry Compton, Mick Stalley and Peter Bishop

392   Tower Captain Rosemary Maclaine and the Bellringers: Mick Stalley, Jean Edwards, Peter Bishop, Terry Compton and Rosemary Maclaine

393   The Church Choir

394   Ralph Jeffries at the Church Gates

395   Anne Warburton at the Org.

396   Ralph Jeffries and the Church Pulpit

397   Josie Hunter at the Organ, St Mary's

399   The Three Grown-Up Sons of Harry Read in Boat Meadow c. 1930:
Wilfred, Charles and Roland

398   The Three Sons of Harry Read
Wilfred *(standing)* Roland *(left)* and Charles

400   Helen Read

401   School Photograph c. 1912 with Harry and Helen Read

402 School Photograph c. 1941

Back Row: Fred Seamarks, Cecil Wooding
Alfred Dawson, Ronald Mitchell, John D
David Wooding, ?

Middle Row: Bernard Dart, Fred Harris,
John Prentice, Rose Woodward, Pam
Cowley, Sue Walton, Victor Tucker, Bill
Harris, John Curtis

Front Row:Leslie Church, Pauline Church
Jill Prentice, Sheila Woods, Beryl Corby,
Cynthia Goldsmith, Betty Markham, ?, P
Walton, Catherine Hodby, Derek Markha

403   School Photograph c. 1960

Back Row: Stephen Beesley, Graham Co
Peter Corby, Jane Cox, Georgina Swain
Pauline Holt, David Harpin, Carol Cox

Second Row: Mrs Parkinson,Stephen Co
Brenda Jeffries, Barbara Mackness, Lin
Crowe, Christine Merrikin, Roy Easton
Harpin, Stephen Jeffries, Miss Lennox.

Third Row: Linda Fisher, Melvin Cox, J
Wildman, Denise Crowe, Jacqueline Pe
Neil Wooding, Geoff Prentice, Phil Dor
Alan Mayes, Colin Aspley.

Front Row: Ian Harris, Ray Cox, Philip
Caroline Fox, Rosemary Keech, Elizabe
Hunter, Marion Cox, Sheila Green, Ang
Curtis

404   School Photograph c. 1965

Back Row: Derek Pearson; Brian Pell; Ste
Jeffries; Steve Cox; David Harpin; Grah
Cox, Melvin Cox

Second Row: Miss Lennox, Ian Harris, C
Aspley, Neil Wooding, Jacqui Pearson, L
Fisher, Carol Cox, Joy Wildman, Alan M
Ray Cox, Keith Seamarks, Mrs Parkinso

Third Row: Kath Keech, Rose Keech, Liz
Hunter, Denise Crowe, Marion Cox, Ang
Curtis, Sheila Green, Valerie Mayes, Kat
Brown

Front Row: Tim Cox, Phil Cox, Lee Harri
Owen Beddoe

406 The Old School Swimming Pool

405 Last Day of School at the Old School

407 The School Bus

408 Marion Watkins

409 Skool or Bussed?

410   The Historical Trust
Back Row: Paul Middleton, Alan Edwards, Peter Hart
Front Row: Peter Stileman, David Stanbridge (Chairman), John Ward

411   Peter Conquest as Cranmer

412   Simon Rockwood and Peter Conquest

413   Stuart Antrobus Lecturing on the Windmill

414
Jerusalem: The WI on Song with Chairwoman Pam Rolls (*Front Row Second from Right*)

415   The Social Centre Committee
Top: Richard Blayney.
Second Row: Iain Morrison (Hon Secretary), Gary Thomas (Chairman)
Front Row: Ged Puckett, Sandra Proud, lison Campion, Brian Westbrook, Barbara Collins, Keith Lee

Chapter 7   Some People

Portraits here of Villagers long gone
Reflect the many trades and pastimes going on,
When people trudged laboriously to work
From dawn to dusk with little chance to shirk
But made their own amusements then as now do we.
Reader read on. Page after page you'll see
Astonishing diversity before your eyes unfold
From cot to grave, both very young and old.

We have few photographs of Villagers for the period before the First World War. Two of the earliest are of Samuel and Jane Harker (nee Burton) **[417 and 416]**. Samuel was a lacemaker, originally from Crowland. He did not personally make lace but collected it from women throughout the Village and surrounding villages who made the lace at home. Their children, Mary Sophia and William Burton Harker, are buried at the Baptist Meeting. The Harkers lived at Yew Tree House on the corner of Silver Street and Park Road. This became one of the Village shops in the early part of the 20th Century. Another early photograph **[422]** shows Marion Field's step-grandfather, Mr Raban, a former owner of the Windmill.

Fortunately, Ray Cox has a unique collection of family photographs going back to his great-grandfather Thomas Cox **[426]** who kept the *Cock Inn* at West End, now a private house. Ray's maternal great-grandfather was William Bowyer **[419]**. His first wife was the redoubtable Rebecca Bowyer **[423]**. Ray's paternal grandfather was Oliver Cox, who kept the *Royal George* after it became a fully-fledged public house. He is seen here with his wife, Lily **[420]**. He was also a saddler and this photograph shows him working at his house in Church Road **[425]. Plate 421** shows him with his whole family. Ray's uncle was Rex Cox (see Chapter 5 **282**). His father, Don Cox, married Marjorie (Madge) Wildman of Felmersham seen in **Plate 428** (right) with her sister, Connie, and in **Plate 418** as a bridesmaid.

In the era of Oliver Cox the Village was much more self-sufficient than now. One can perhaps understand why we no longer have a saddler, but when so much riding goes on locally the loss of the smithy is a shame. One of the last blacksmiths was Dick Ruffhead of Silver Street (see Chapter 3 **137**). Only two followed him, and the smithy in Church Road closed in the late 1960s. Until recently, the gap was filled by a peripatetic farrier, Michael ("Tubbs") Chisholm **[472]**. In the last three decades we have lost the Village School (1983), the Bakery in Silver Street and the adjoining shop (1971-3) as well as the corner shop at the Cross which closed in 1994 after two armed raids. George Strong and his late wife Phyllis ran the latter shop for many years. The last shopkeepers were Brian and Liz Stammers **[462]**. Both have been active in the Sailing Club for some time and Liz has also served on the Social Centre Committee. The gap left by the closure of the shop was filled in part by the initiative of Jacqui Ward, Sarah Bush and others who established the Community Shop which thrives in the Church Rooms **[441]**. It celebrated its tenth anniversary this year **[442]**.

Fortunately, we still have a Post Office and **Plate 445** shows the postmistress, Tracey Bailey, with the regular post lady, Gill King **[447]**, and her relief, Jean Blayney. Stan Walker supplied the Village with newspapers until 1985 **[446]**. He was head groundsman at the Bedford Modern School until 1982. He is seen in **Plate 444** with HM The Queen at the opening of the School's new buildings in 1973. He says she told him to look after the tree as she did not have green fingers. Stan's own garden is still a picture **[457]**, but there is enough grass for two of him. The last milk delivery from the Village was in the late 1980s when the Homers called it a day.

While self-sufficiency may seem to be in decline, many essential services are still supplied locally. Charlie Finch plumbs and heats the Village (see Chapter 5 **333**). Mickey Garrett (aka "The Biddler"), a daytime refugee from Pavenham, is progressively rebuilding the Village and is seen here **[437]** with his Clerk of Works, Bill Wills-Moren, and assistant bricklayer Nick Finch. Mick Stalley has repainted the Village and John Geerts (aka "Poisson"), captured here with a recent catch **[474]**, supplies us with fresh fish; Magnus Lennie and his lads **[473]** keep our gardens tidy. Stephanie Field is a qualified homoeopath [476].

Robert Shaftoe's workshop in the old Primitive Methodist Chapel is always a source of interest. It is there that he builds and renovates organs and manufactures harpsichords and spinets [478]. David Litchfield [477] has his own coach business (see Chapter 5 295), and Litchy's coach has taken Villagers all over Britain and Europe on various jaunts and holidays, not to mention booze cruises to the Pas de Calais.

The Village is fortunate in its musicians and always has been. Philip Bond (see Chapter 5 324), Liz Cox (see Chapter 5 325), Joan Hart (see Chapter 5 322), Terry and Marion Hext [459], Dita Hollins (see Chapter 5 345) and Ann Warburton (see Chapter 6 395) have all taught locally, but the Village has had the benefit of their skills in many concerts and revues. A surprising number of Village children play an instrument and almost at the drop of a hat it seems possible to conjure up an orchestra or a choir.

The Hexts' elder son, Michael Hext [460], was BBC Young Musician of the Year in 1978. After college he joined the Covent Garden orchestra and his brother, David [461], joined the Halle orchestra as a percussionist.

Indeed, in Stevington people have never existed in a vacuum. It has long been a Village of clubs and associations. Inevitably they come and go. For example, the Flower Club [424], in which Mary Mackness was a leading light and honorary secretary, exists no more. It revived in the 1990s for a brief period as the Gardening Club through the efforts of Roger Disson and Bob Poulter. The apogee was a ten-minute slot on *Gardener's World*. A seed-buying cooperative still survives. The Stevington Investment Club, "Spike Island", was wound up this year after some exciting years of speculation under the chairmanship of Alan Proud [464]. The Youth Club, despite much dedicated effort, closed in 2001.

On the other hand, the Stevington Brownies are a well-established group and have maintained a vital focus for Stevington's young ladies over the years. They are seen here in action in **Plates 432 and 433**. The longest serving Brown Owl was the late Janet Litchfield [435], but Jackie Gooding, who succeeded her, is set to equal her record [434]. The nursery school at the Manse under the leadership of Brigid Cox [429] is moulding the new generation and turning the girls, at least, into suitable candidates for the Brownies. The Summer School [431] which she also organises is always oversubscribed.

Other individuals make outstanding personal contributions on their own account. One of these is Pat Pickup who has edited the Village Magazine since 1987, latterly with the assistance of her husband, Ian [436]. We shall greatly miss the work of the Village genealogist, Helen Allen, who died last year (2003). She traced the genealogies of some 24 Stevington families and the Historical Trust has custody of her archive [458].

Other Villagers pursue interesting hobbies. That of Simon and Kathy Brown [448] at the Manor House is a major undertaking. They have created what is undoubtedly the finest garden ever seen in the Village and one that is part of the National Gardens Scheme [449-56]. Visitors regularly come from abroad to view it. Kathy is a qualified garden designer. The Jubilee celebrations in 2002 were held there in a splendid setting.

But they are not alone. For example, Aleks Murzyn flies a helicopter [469] and formerly was the world individual hovercraft champion, while Mary and Brian Webb build dolls' houses [471].

A rather different contribution is made by the Village's own middle-aged pop stars, the Snarling Beasties. The group comprises a teacher, two aeronautical technicians and a solicitor. They never fail to entertain, but despite their professional expertise they are still aiming for a hit (see Chapter 5 337).

Our final pictures are of the youngest Villager, Connor Cox, born this year [483] and the oldest, Violet Warwick, aged 100 [482]. She has since celebrated yet another birthday.

STEVINGTON MAGAZINE

SEPTEMBER 2004
Number 130

416   Jane Harker b. 16 October 1834   417   Samuel Harker b. 3 January 1828

418   Madge Cox as a Bridesmaid   419   William Bowyer with Thomas Bolton   420   Oliver and Lily Cox

421   Oliver Cox and Family   422   Marion Field's Step-Grandfather, Mr Raban

424   The Flower Club

423   Rebecca Bowyer

425   Oliver Cox as Saddler

426   Thomas Cox

427   William Hensman Robinson of Hart Farm with his Wife

428   Connie and Her Sister Madge

429 Children of the Ma... Nursery School

430 Summer Playgroup 1989

431 Summer School 2004

432   Brownies' Tableau

433   Brownies' Attack

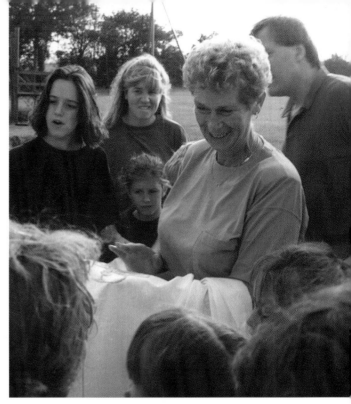

434　Jackie Gooding

435　Janet Litchfield

436　Pat and Ian Pickup

437　On Site: Bill Wills-
Moren, Mick Garrett and
Nick Finch

438   The South Orbital Sewer Cometh

439   Surfacing

Disposal

441   The Community Shop: Café au Lait
June Homer, Jacqui Ward, Janet Day, Carol Woods and Doreen Pendlington

442   The Community Shop: Tenth Anniversary
Sandra Proud, Doreen Pendlington, June Homer, Jacqui Ward, Tom Batty and Sarah Bush

Alan Edwards with HRH The Duke of Edinburgh

444   Stan Walker with the HM The Queen

445   The Mail Fists: Jean Blayney, Gill King and Tracey Bailey

446   Stan Walker on his Delivery Bike

447   Pony Express

448   Simon and Kathy Brown

449   Trailing a Path Through
the French Garden

449-456
Manor House Garden

450   The Manor House

451   The Tiered Garden

452
The Old Fish Pond, Now
with Summer Succulents and
Exotics

453
Bridal Rose Arch

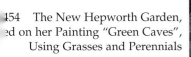

454   The New Hepworth Garden,
ed on her Painting "Green Caves",
Using Grasses and Perennials

455 Red Rosa "Parkdirector Riggers" and Blue Clematis "Prince Charles" make a Wonderful Summer Planting Scheme

456 Lofty Spires of Brilliant Blue Delphiniums Thrive on the Rich Clay Soil

457 Stan Walker and His Twin Brother

458   Helen Allen

459   Terry and Marion Hext

460   Michael Hext:
The First BBC Young Musician of the Year 1978

461   David Hext

462   Brian and Liz Stammers

463   Rob and Ged Puckett

464   Alan and Sandra Proud

465   Jim Keech with the New Windmill Sails

466   Frank Wooding at Hart Farm

467   Roy Pryn with the Church Key

468   Marina and Albert Markham with the 1936 Alvis Crested Eagle

469   Aleks Murzyn with his Choppers

470   Marion Field at the Well

471   Mary and Brian Webb

472   Michael ("Tubbs") Chisholm, the Farrier

473   Magnus Lennie and his Lads

474   John Geerts Angling for a Sale

475   Rob Puckett on Pike Drill

479   Chris Boniface as Moses among the Bullrushes

478   Robert Shaftoe in his Workshop

481 Promenade

482 Violet Warwick aged 100

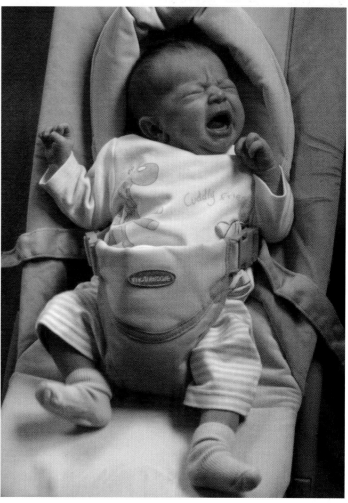

483 Connor Cox aged 14 Days

Stevington, Goodnight!

Last Reader, Turn Out the Light!

Index of Proper Names

References in plain text refer to the page number; references in bold refer to the plate number. Nicknames are bracketed.

Peter Hart Engaged in Essential Fieldwork for this Publication